1001

JOKES 4 KIDS

1001

JOKES 4 KIDS

Jokes & Riddles, Knock Knocks, Limericks, Tongue Twisters

& So Much More!

GRAHAM CANN

Chas Cann Publishers

CONTENTS

LUDICROUS LIMERICKS

There was a young lady of Ryde,
Whose shoe-strings were seldom untied.
She purchased some clogs,
And some spotty dogs,
And frequently strode in a stride.

There once was a Martian named Zed,
With antennae all over his head.
He sent out a lot
of di-di-dash-dot,
But nobody knows what he said.

I know a young fellow named Vin,
Who is really remarkably thin.
When he carries a pole,
People say "Bless my soul,
What a shock to find out you've a twin".

There was once a farmer from Leeds,
Who swallowed a packet of seeds.
It soon came to pass,
He was covered with grass,
But has all the tomatoes he needs.

A creature of charm is the gerbil,
It's diet's exclusively herbal.
It grazes all day,
On bunches of hay,
Passing gas with an elegant burble.

There once was a man from Peru,
Who dreamed that he swallowed his shoe.
He woke up in fright,
In the middle of the night,
To learn that his dream had come true!

A funny young fellow named Perkins,
Was terribly fond of small gherkins.
One day after tea,
He ate ninety-three,
And pickled his internal workings!

A tutor who tooted a flute,
Tried to teach two young tooters to toot.
Said the two to the tutor,
"Is it harder to toot, or....
To tutor two tooters to toot?"

An extremely slim model, Miss Slater,
Was attacked by a croc and it ate 'er,
Said her trainer, "Tough deal!
What a horrible meal -
We should throw it some greens and potaters."

A canner, exceedingly canny,
One morning remarked to his granny,
"A canner can can
Anything that he can,
But a canner can't can a can, can he?"

There was a man from Dealing
Who caught the bus for Ealing.
It said on the door,
"Don't spit on the floor."
So he jumped up and spat on the ceiling.

There was a young fellow who thought,
Very little, but thought it a lot.
Then at long last he knew,
What he wanted to do,
But before he could start, he forgot!

An elderly man called Keith
Mislaid his set of false teeth.
They'd been laid on a chair
He'd forgot they were there
Sat down and was bitten beneath.

There once was a Thingamijig -
Like a Whatsis, but three times as big.
When it first came in view,
It looked something like you,
But it stayed and turned into a pig!

There was once a hunter named Paul,
Who strangled nine grizzlies one fall.
Nine is such a good score,
So he tried for one more,
But he lost. Well, you can't win them all!

Speedy Sam, while exploring a cave,
Had what I call a very close shave.
He stepped on a bear,
That had dozed off in there.
I'm glad he was faster than brave.

There were once two back-country geezers,
Who got porcupine quills up their sneezers.
They sat beak to beak,
For more than a week,
Working over each other with tweezers.

Limericks I cannot compose,
With noxious smells in my nose.
But this one is easy,
I only felt queasy,
Because I was sniffing my toes.

There once was a man named Brice,
Who had a nasty head full of lice.
He said, "If I eat them,
Then I'll have beat them!
And besides, they taste very nice!"

There was a young lady of Cork,
Whose pa made a fortune in pork.
He bought for his daughter,
A tutor who taught her,
To balance green peas on her fork.

There once was a man from Tibet,
Who couldn't find a cigarette.
So he smoked all his socks,
And got chicken-pox,
So had to go to the vet.

A painter, who lived in Great Britain,
Interrupted two girls with their knitting,
He said, with a sigh,
"That park bench, well I,
Just painted it, right where you're sitting."

An ambitious young fellow named Matt,
Tried to parachute using his hat.
Folks below looked so small,
As he started to fall.
Then got bigger and bigger –
and SPLATT!!

There was a young lady of Kent,
Whose nose was most awfully bent.
She followed her nose,
One day, I suppose,
And no-one knows which way she went.

There once was a man from York,
Who picked his nose with a fork.
He went for a pluck,
When it got right stuck,
It didn't half make him squawk!

The incredible Wizard of Oz,
Retired from his business becoz.
Due to up-to-date science,
To most of his clients,
He wasn't the Wizard he woz.

There is a young schoolboy named Mason,
Whose mom cuts his hair with a basin.
When he stands in one place,
With a scarf round his face,
It's a mystery which way he's facing.

A young gourmet dining at Crewe,
Found a rather large mouse in his stew.
Said the waiter, "Don't shout,
And wave it about,
Or the rest will be wanting one too."

There was a young lady named Rose,
Who had a large wart on her nose.
When she had it removed,
Her appearance improved,
But her glasses slipped down to her toes.

Our school trip was a special occasion,
But we never reached our destination.
Instead of the zoo,
I was locked in the loo,
Of the toilet at the service station!

There was a bold pirate of Boulder,
Whose cutlass was slung from his shoulder.
He'd mighty fine notions,
Of plundering oceans,
But his mom said: "Perhaps, when you're older."

There once was a nice Easter bunny,
He hopped around looking quite funny.
He injured his leg,
While holding an egg,
Then he didn't feel very sunny.

There once was a girl in the choir,
Whose voice rose up hoir and hoir,
Till it reached such a height,
It went clear out of sight,
And they found it next day in the spoir!

There was a young schoolboy of Rye,
Who was placed by mistake in a pie.
To his mother's disgust,
He emerged through the crust,
And exclaimed, with a yawn, "Where am I?"

"I talk," claimed a linguist named Hamill,
"With every species of mammal."
When asked for a reference,
He said, "What's your preference?
My mother-in-law, or my camel?"

Sunbaking one day on a rock,
A lizard was in for a shock.
A bird hunting prey,
Whisked his tail clear away!
Poor stumpy is still taking stock.

The bicycling poodle he saw,
Made the cop on the beat drop his jaw.
It was easy to tell,
That it rode rather well,
Though its hand signals were rather paw.

A mouse in the room woke Miss Dowd,
She was frightened, it must be allowed.
Soon a happy thought hit her,
To scare off the critter,
She sat up in bed and meowed.

A circus performer named Brian
Once smiled as he rode on a lion.
They came back from the ride
But with Brian inside
And the smile on the face of the lion.

A flea and a fly in a flue,
Were imprisoned, so what could they do?
Said the fly, "Let us flee!"
"Let us fly!" said the flea.
So they flew through a flaw in the flue.

There was once a baby named Lou,
And he grew and he grew and he grew,
And he grew and he grew,
And he grew and he grew.
But he stopped when he reached six foot two.

An elephant slept in his bunk,
And in slumber his chest rose and sunk,
But he snored - how he snored!
All the other beasts roared.
So his wife tied a knot in his trunk.

There was once a girl who said "How,
Shall I manage to carry my cow?
Every time that I ask it,
to get in my basket,
It makes such a terrible row!"

I needed a front door for my hall,
The replacement I bought was too tall.
So I hacked it and chopped it,
And carefully lopped it.
And now the darn thing is too small.

Amazingly, antelope stew,
Is supposedly better for you,
Than goulash of rat,
Or Hungarian cat,
But I guess, that was something you knew.

There was an old man with a beard,
Who said, "It's just as I feared,
Two owls and a hen,
Four larks and a wren,
Have all built their nests in my beard!"

There was an old man in a tree,
Who was horribly bored by a bee.
When they said, "Does it buzz?"
He said, "Yes it does!
It's a regular brute of a bee!"

There once was an ape in a zoo,
Who looked through the bars and saw YOU!
Do you think it's fair,
To give poor apes a scare?
I think it's a mean think to do.

Tim wore rubberbands on his wrist,
For each item on his to-do list.
But the more he forgot,
The bigger it got,
So now it's a big rubber fist!

A wonderful bird is the pelican,
His bill can hold more than his beli-can.
He can take in his beak
Enough food for the week,
But I'm darned if I see how the heli-can.

There was a snowman called Ray,
Who was having a lovely day,
Until it started to get sunny,
And he became all runny,
Then sadly Ray melted away.

NATTY KNOCK KNOCKS

Knock, knock,
Who's there?
A broken pencil.
A broken pencil, who?
Never mind, it's pointless!

Knock, knock,
Who's there?
A herd.
A herd, who?
A herd you were home, so here I am!

Knock, knock,
Who's there?
A little old lady.
A little old lady, who?
Didn't know you could yodel!

Knock, knock,
Who's there?
Aardvark.
Aardvark who?
Aardvark a million miles for one of your smiles!

Knock, knock,
Who's there?
Bacon.
Bacon who?
Bacon a cake for your birthday!

Knock, knock,
Who's there?
Barbara.
Barbara who?
Barbara black sheep have you any wool?

Knock, knock,
Who's there?
Candice.
Candice who?
Candice knock-knock jokes get any better?

Knock, knock,
Who's there?
Dishes.
Dishes who?
Dishes the police! Open up!

Knock, knock,
Who's there?
Abbey.
Abbey who?
Abbey stung me on the nose!

Knock, knock,
Who's there?
Avenue.
Avenue who?
Avenue knocked on this door before?

Knock, knock,
Who's there?
Doris.
Doris who?
Door is locked, that's why I'm knocking!

Knock, knock,
Who's there?
I am.
I am who?
Don't you even know who you are?

Knock, knock,
Who's there?
Ice cream.
Ice cream who?
Ice cream if you don't give me some candy!

Knock, knock,
Who's there?
Kanga.
Kanga who?
No, it's kangaroo!

Knock, knock,
Who's there?
Giraffe.
Giraffe who?
Giraffe anything to eat? I'm hungry!

Knock, knock,
Who's there?
Keith.
Keith who?
Keith me my thweet printh!

Knock, knock,
Who's there?
Leaf.
Leaf who?
Leaf me alone!

Knock, knock,
Who's there?
Needle.
Needle who?
Needle little help right now!

Knock, knock,
Who's there?
Olive.
Olive who?
Olive you sooooo much!

Knock, knock,
Who's there?
Police.
Police who?
Police let me in, it's chilly out!

Knock, knock,
Who's there?
Sadie.
Sadie who?
Sadie magic word and I'll disappear!

Knock, knock,
Who's there?
A wood wok.
A wood wok who?
A wood wok 500 miles, and a wood wok 500 more!

Knock, knock,
Who's there?
Thumpin'.
Thumpin' who?
There's thumpin' furry crawling up your back!

Knock, knock,
Who's there?
Voodoo.
Voodoo who?
Voodoo you think you are?

Knock, knock,
Who's there?
Who.
Who who?
I didn't know you were an owl?

Knock, knock,
Who's there?
Zinc.
Zinc who?
Zinc or swim!

Knock, knock,
Who's there?
Abbott.
Abbott who?
Abbott you don't know who this is?

Knock, knock,
Who's there?
Amarillo.
Amarillo who?
Amarillo nice person!

Knock, knock,
Who's there?
Barry.
Barry who?
Barry nice to see you!

Knock, knock,
Who's there?
Cash.
Cash who?
No thanks, I prefer peanuts!

Knock, knock,
Who's there?
Abby.
Abby who?
Abby birthday to you!

Knock, knock,
Who's there?
Cereal.
Cereal who?
Cereal pleasure to meet you!

Knock, Knock,

Who's there?

Canoe.

Canoe who?

Canoe come out and play?

Knock, knock,
Who's there?
Ben.
Ben who?
Ben knocking for 10 minutes!

Knock, knock,
Who's there?
Doughnut.
Doughnut who?
Doughnut ask, it's a secret!

Knock, knock,
Who's there?
Ears.
Ears who?
Ears another knock-knock joke for ya!

Knock, knock,
Who's there?
Figs.
Figs who?
Figs the doorbell, it's not working!

Knock, knock,
Who's there?
Goliath.
Goliath who?
Goliath down, you look-eth tired!

Knock, knock,
Who's there?
Harry.
Harry who?
Harry up, it's cold outside!

Knock, knock,
Who's there?
Icing.
Icing who?
Icing so loud, the neighbours can hear me!

Knock, knock,
Who's there?
Juicy.
Juicy who?
Juicy what I saw?

Knock, knock,
Who's there?
Ken.
Ken who?
Ken I come in? It's freezing out here!

Knock, knock,
Who's there?
Mary.
Mary who?
Mary Christmas!

Knock, knock,
Who's there?
Noah.
Noah who?
Noah good place we can go to hang out?

Knock, knock,
Who's there?
Organ.
Organ who?
Organ-ize a party, it's my birthday!

Knock, knock,
Who's there?
Says.
Says who?
Says me!

Knock, knock,
Who's there?
Scold.
Scold who?
Scold enough out here to go ice skating!

Knock, knock,
Who's there?
Turnip.
Turnip who?
Turnip the volume, I love this song!

Knock, knock,
Who's there?
Viper.
Viper who?
Viper nose, it's running!

Knock, knock,
Who's there?
Watson.
Watson who?
Watson TV right now?

Knock, knock,
Who's there?
Accordion.
Accordion who?
Accordion to the weather forecast, it's going to rain!

Knock, Knock,
Who's there?
Stopwatch.
Stopwatch who?
Stopwatch you're doing and let me in!

Knock, knock,
Who's there?
Water.
Water who?
Water you doing telling jokes right now?
Don't you have better things to do?

Knock, knock,
Who's there?
Boo.
Boo who?
There's no need to cry!

Knock, knock,
Who's there?
Ada.
Ada who?
Ada burger for lunch!

Knock, knock,
Who's there?
Cargo.
Cargo who?
No, car-go Beep! Beep!

Knock, knock,
Who's there?
Adore.
Adore who?
Adore is between us, so open it!

Knock, knock,
Who's there?
Amos.
Amos who?
Amos Quito!

Knock, knock,
Who's there?
Cheese.
Cheese who?
Cheese such a sweet girl!

Knock, knock,
Who's there?
Egbert.
Egbert who?
Egbert no bacon please!

Knock, knock,
Who's there?
Cher.
Cher who?
Cher would be nice if you opened the door!

Knock, Knock,
Who's there?
Cow says.
Cow says who?
No, a cow says moooo!

Knock, knock,
Who's there?
Foster.
Foster who?
Foster than a speeding bullet!

Knock, knock,
Who's there?
Four eggs.
Four eggs who?
Four eggs-ample it's me!

Knock, knock,
Who's there?
Gus.
Gus who?
Gus how old I am today?

Knock, knock,
Who's there?
Hatch.
Hatch who?
Bless you!

Knock, knock,
Who's there?
Hawaii.
Hawaii who?
I'm good, Hawaii you?

Knock, knock,
Who's there?
Icy.
Icy who?
Icy you looking at me!

Knock, knock,
Who's there?
Al.
Al who?
Al give you a hug if you open this door!

Knock, knock,
Who's there?
Alec.
Alec who?
Alectricity. BUZZ!!

Knock, knock,
Who's there?
Stu.
Stu who?
Stu late, it's time for bed!

Knock, knock,
Who's there?
Theodore.
Theodore who?
Theodore is stuck. That's why I'm knocking!

Knock, Knock,
Who's there?
Theresa.
Theresa who?
Theresa fly in my soup!

Knock, knock,
Who's there?
Weirdo.
Weirdo who?
Weirdo you think you're going?

Knock, knock,
Who's there?
Wendy.
Wendy who?
Wendy bell works again, I won't have to knock!

Knock, knock,
Who's there?
Yukon.
Yukon who?
Yukon say that again!

Knock, knock,
Who's there?
Alex.
Alex who?
Alex-plain later!

Knock, knock,
Who's there?
Claire.
Claire who?
Claire a path, I'm coming through!

Knock, knock,
Who's there?
Dozen.
Dozen who?
Dozen anyone want to let me in?

Knock, knock,
Who's there?
Emma.
Emma who?
Emma getting hungry. What's for dinner?

Knock, knock,
Who's there?
Gladys.
Gladys who?
Gladys the weekend!

Knock, knock,
Who's there?
Goat.
Goat who?
Go to the door and you'll find out!

Knock, knock,
Who's there?
Ho-ho.
Ho-ho who?
Your Santa impersonation could do with a little work!

Knock, knock,
Who's there?
Hugo.
Hugo who?
Hugo first! I'm right behind you!

Knock, knock,
Who's there?
Iona.
Iona who?
Iona new toy!

Knock, knock,
Who's there?
Lettuce.
Lettuce who?
Lettuce in, it's cold our here!

Knock, knock,
Who's there?
Kent.
Kent who?
Kent you tell who I am from my voice?

Knock, Knock,
Who's there?
Ashe.
Ashe who?
Bless you!

Knock, knock,
Who's there?
Nana.
Nana who?
Nana your business!

Knock, knock,
Who's there?
Pecan.
Pecan who?
Pecan somebody your own size!

Knock, knock,
Who's there?
Tank.
Tank who?
You're welcome!

Knock, knock,
Who's there?
Woo.
Woo who?
Glad you're excited too!

Knock, knock,
Who's there?
Robin.
Robin who?
Robin you! Now hand over the cash!

Knock, knock,
Who's there?
Scott.
Scott who?
Scott nothing to do with you!

Knock, knock,
Who's there?
Art.
Art who?
R2-D2, of course!

Knock, knock,
Who's there?
Dwayne.
Dwayne who?
Dwayne the bath, I'm drowning!

Knock, knock,
Who's there?
Eyesore.
Eyesore who?
Eyesore from my long run - can we take the elevator?

Knock, knock,
Who's there?
Haden.
Haden who?
Haden seek!

Knock, Knock,
Who's there?
Honeybee.
Honeybee who?
Honey bee good!

Knock, knock,
Who's there?
Alex.
Alex who?
Hey, Alex the questions around here!

Knock, knock,
Who's there?
Etch.
Etch who?
Bless you!

Knock, knock,
Who's there?
Hal.
Hal who?
Hal will you know if you don't open the door!

Knock, knock,
Who's there?
Ike.
who?
Ike could have danced all night!

Knock, knock,
Who's there?
Ketchup.
Ketchup who?
Ketchup with me and I'll tell you!

Knock, knock,
Who's there?
Kirtch.
Kirtch who?
God bless you!

Knock, knock,
Who's there?
Justin.
Justin who?
Justin time for dinner!

Knock, knock,
Who's there?
Mikey.
Mikey who?
Mikey doesn't fit in the keyhole!

Knock, knock,
Who's there?
Nobel.
Nobel who?
Nobel.... that's why I knocked!

Knock, knock,
Who's there?
Pete.
Pete who?
Pete-za delivery!

Knock, knock,
Who's there?
Seed.
Seed who?
Seed you tomorrow!

Knock, knock,
Who's there?
Spell.
Spell who?
W.H.O.

Knock, knock,
Who's there?
Wooden shoe.
Wooden shoe who?
Wooden shoe like to hear another joke?

Knock, knock,
Who's there?
Yah.
Yah who?
No, I prefer Google!

Knock, knock,
Who's there?
Alice.
Alice who?
Alice fair in love and war!

Knock, knock,
Who's there?
Annie.
Annie who?
Annie thing you can do, I can do better!

Knock, knock,
Who's there?
Honeydew.
Honeydew who?
Honey-dew wanna dance?

**Knock, knock,
Who's there?
Europe.
Europe who?
No, you're a poo!**

Knock, Knock,
Who's there?
Althea.
Althea who?
Althea later, alligator!

Knock, knock,
Who's there?
Ireland.
Ireland who?
Ireland you my umbrella, you're going to need it!

Knock, knock,
Who's there?
Luke.
Luke who?
Luke through the letterbox and find out!

Knock, knock,
Who's there?
Alpaca.
Alpaca who?
Alpaca trunk, you packa suitcase!

Knock, knock,
Who's there?
Anita.
Anita who?
Anita borrow something!

Knock, knock,
Who's there?
Howl.
Howl who?
Howl you know unless you open the door?

**Knock, knock,
Who's there?
Iris.
Iris who?
Iris you'd sing me a song!**

Knock, knock,
Who's there?
Anee.
Anee who?
Anee one you like!

**Knock, knock,
Who's there?
Isabelle.
Isabelle who?
Isabelle necessary on a bicycle?**

Knock, knock,
Who's there?
Norma Lee.
Norma Lee who?
Norma Lee I don't go around knocking on doors!

Knock, knock,
Who's there?
Ray.
Ray who?
Ray-member me?!

Knock, knock,
Who's there?
Iva.
Iva who?
Iva sore hand from knocking!

Knock, knock,
Who's there?
Muffin.
Muffin who?
Muffin the matter with me, how about you?

Knock, knock,
Who's there?
Razor.
Razor who?
Razor hands, this is a stick up!

Knock, knock,
Who's there?
Thermos.
Thermos who?
Thermos be a better way to get to you!

Knock, Knock,
Who's there?
Snow.
Snow who?
Snow use. The joke is over!

Knock, knock,
Who's there?
Sensei.
Sensei who?
I sensei bad joke coming!

Knock, knock,
Who's there?
Ivor.
Ivor who?
Ivor you let me in or I'll climb through the window!

Knock, knock,
Who's there?
Tennis.
Tennis who?
Tennis five plus five!

Knock, knock,
Who's there?
Soup.
Soup who?
Souperwoman!

Knock, knock,
Who's there?
Broccoli.
Broccoli who?
Broccoli doesn't have a last name!

Knock, knock who's there?
Mustache.
Mustache who?
I mustache you a question.

TROUBLESOME TONGUE TWISTERS

"If two witches were watching two watches: which witch would watch which watch?"

**"Cute cookie cutter cut cute cookies,
if cute cookie cutter cut cute cookies
how many cute cookies
can a cute cookie cutter cut?"**

"How many cookies could a good cook cook
If a good cook could cook cookies?
A good cook could cook as much cookies
as a good cook who could cook cookies."

"Rory's lawn rake rarely rakes really right."

"Rory the warrior
and Roger the worrier
were reared wrongly
in a rural brewery."

**"Six sick hicks
nick six slick bricks
with picks and sticks."**

"If one doctor doctors another doctor,
then which doctor is doctoring the doctored doctor?
Does the doctor who doctors the doctor,
doctor the doctor the way the doctor
he is doctoring doctors?"

**"How many yaks
could a yak pack,
pack if a yak pack
could pack yaks?"**

"She sells seashells on the seashore.
The shells she sells are seashells, I'm sure.
And if she sells seashells on the seashore,
then I'm sure she sells seashore shells."

**"I scream,
you scream,
we all scream
for ice cream"**

A skunk sat on a stump and thunk the stump stunk, but the stump thunk the skunk stunk.

"Sixth sick sheik's sixth sheep's sick."

**"The bottom of the butter bucket
is the buttered bucket bottom."**

"Whether the weather is warm,
whether the weather is hot,
we have to put up with the weather,
whether we like it or not."

**"Give papa
a cup of proper
coffee in a
copper coffee cup."**

"I saw Susie sitting in a shoe shine shop.
Where she shines, she sits,
and where she sits, she shines."

"How much dew does a dewdrop drop.
If dewdrops do drop dew?
As do dewdrops drop,
if dewdrops do drop dew."

"If a black bug bleeds black blood, what colour blood does a blue bug bleed?"

"I thought a thought,
but the thought I thought
wasn't the thought I thought I thought.
If the thought I thought I thought
had been the thought I thought,
then I wouldn't have thought so much."

"Denise seizes the fleece.
Denise sees the fleas.
At least Denise could sneeze and feed and freeze the fleas."

"If a dog chews shoes, whose shoes does he choose?"

Five frantic frogs fled from fifty fierce fishes.

"She sold six shabby sheared sheep on a ship."

BONKERS BOOK TITLES

A Day in the Saddle by Major Bumsore

A History of Welsh Comedians by Dai Laffyn

Batman's Enemy by Joe Kerr

Call the Police! by Laura Norda

Danger! by Luke Out

Geology by Roxanne Minerals

Blushing by Rosie Cheeks

Carpet Fitting by Walter Wall

Dentist at Work by Phil McCavity

Eat As Much Food As You Like by I. M. A. Piggee

Desserts by Sue Flay

Falling Knickers by Lucy Lastic

Full Moon by Seymour Bottom

I Lost my Balance by Eileen Dover and Paul Down

Horrendous by Terry Bull

Hot Dog! by Frank Furter

Advantageous by Ben E Fishall

Common Allergies by P. Nutt

Falling Trees by Tim Burr

I Didn't Do It by Ivan Alibi

It's a Hold Up! By Nick R. Elastic

Mega Bites by Amos Quito

Staying Calm by Terry Fide

Sinking Ships by Mandy Pumps

The Butter Debate by Marge Isbetter

The Leaky Tap by Constant Dripping

Turkish Fast Food by Donna K Bab

After School Agony by Dee Tension

Brown Trousers by Di Rear

Cloning by Imma Dubble 11

I Hate the Sun by Gladys Knight

Flying Dinosaur by Tara Dactyll

All Day on My Sofa by I Doolittle

Almost Missed the Bus by Justin Time

Cloud Burst by Wayne Drops

Red Vegetables by B. Troot

Fatal Illness by Ann Thrax

French Cookery by Sue Flay

Something Fishy by Ann Chovy

Pancakes by Mabel Sirrup

Salad Dressing by May O'Naise

70

Old Age by Jerry Attrick

Make Your Own Honey by B Keeper

Never Forget by L. E. Phant

Kings and Queens by Roy Altee

It's Unfair by Y. Mee

I've Got All I Need by E. Nuff

Mensa Man by Gene Yuss

Robots by Anne Droid

Late Again by Misty Buss

The Great British Breakfast by Chris P. Bacon

Vegetable Gardening by Rosa Cabbages

Crumbs in my Cuppa by Duncan Biscuits

Waiting in Line for the Bathroom by Ivana Tinkle

Amphibians by Newt & Sally Mander

Antibiotics by Penny Silling

Collection Litter by Phil D Basket

Crossing Roads Safely by Luke Bothways.

Flipping Great Waves by Sue Nahmi

Golly Gosh by G. Whizz

Good Housekeeping by Lottie Dust

I Need Insurance by Justin Case

I Say So! By Frank O. Pinion

Fun on Two Wheels by Sy Cling

Getting Started by Mo Mentum

Errors and Accidents by Miss Takes and Miss Haps

How to Become a Statue by Stan Still

Lion Taming by Claude Bottom

Rowing in the Pacific by Willie Maykit

Chicken
Dishes

By
Nora
Drumstick

Art & Culture by Phyllis Stein

Artificial Clothing by Polly Ester

How Hurricanes Start by Gustav Wind

Sunday Service by Neil Downe

The Big Bang by Dina Mite

Poked in the Eye by Dee Stick

Off to Market by Tobias A Pig

Smelly Breath by Hal E. Tosis

Rusty Bedsprings by I.P. Knightly

Hair Disorders by Dan Druff

Cat's Revenge by Claude Balls

Bubbles in the Bath by Ivor Windybottom

Laser Weapon by Rae Gunn

Learning to Read by Abe E. Seas

The Meaning of Words by Dick Shunnry

Winning the Race by Vic Tree

There's a Hole in my Bucket by Lee King

The Prisoner's Been Let Out by Freda Convict

Without Warning By Oliver Sudden

I Can't Stand Straight by Ilene Over

I Was a Cloakroom Attendant by Mahatma Coate

Bullfighting by Matt Adore

Covered Walkways by R. Kade

Sore Joints by A King

Looking Younger by Fay Slift

Diamonds Are A Girl's Best Friend by Jules Sparkle

Discovering Islands by Archie Pelago

Hair Today, Gone Tomorrow by I.M. Balding

I'm Fine by Howard Yu

Improve your Garden by Anita Lawn

Easy Money by Robin Banks

Excitement by Hugh N. Cry

French Overpopulation by Francis Crowded

Highway Travel By Dusty Rhodes

Living with Mosquito Bites by Ivana Scratch

Outdoor Activities by Alf Fresco

Over the Cliff by Hugo First

Large Snakes by Anna Conda

Lion Attack by Claudia Armoff

Living Through the Storm by Ty Foon

Seaside Treats by Rhoda Donkey

Shipwrecked by Mandy Lifeboats

Stone Age by Neil Ithic

The Arctic Ocean by I.C. Waters

Dogs Dinner by Nora Bone

Working Out by Jim Nasium

Will He Win by Betty Wont

Showing Guts by N Trayles

The Yellow River by I.P Daily

The End of the World by Major Disaster

Truancy by Marcus Absent

Mosquito Bites by Ivan Itch

Not Too Hot, Not Too Cold by Lou Quarm

Scouting for Boys by Ivor Woggle

Surprised! By Omar Gosh

The Facts About Sun Care Lotion by Justin Casey Burns

Things Girls Cannot Do by B. A. Boy

Tug of War by Paul Hard

No-One Knows My Name by Ima Nonnymous

Smashing Shellfish by Buster Crabbe

Telephone Problems by Ron Number

The Future of Robotics by Cy Borg and Anne Droid

Walking in Circles by Ilene Wright

Touch Your Toes for Fitness by Ben Dover

Why Should I Walk? By Iona Carr

Understanding Algebra by Percy Vere

Transport in the Middle Ages by Orson Carte

Voice Amplification by Mike Raphone

ANIMAL CRACKERS

How do you catch a squirrel chimp? Climb up a tree and act like a nut!

A monkey, a squirrel and a bird are racing to the top of a coconut tree. Who will get the banana first - the monkey, the squirrel or the bird? None of them because you can't get a banana from a coconut tree.

Can a kangaroo jump higher than the Empire State Building? Of course! The Empire State Building can't jump!

I told my friend that I saw a moose on the way to work this morning. She said 'How do you know he was on his way to work?'

What always sleeps with its shoes on?
A horse.

What do you get when you cross a Cocker Spaniel with a poodle and a rooster? A cockapoodledoo!

What goes zzub zzub?
A bee flying backwards.

How do you hire a horse?
Stand it on four bricks.

What time is it when a hippopotamus sits on your hat?
Time to get a new hat!

When is it bad luck to see a black cat?
When you are a mouse.

Why are seagulls called
seagulls?
Because if they flew over the
bay, they'd be bagels!

Where do horses go when they're sick?
Horsepital.

Why did the crab get arrested?
Because he was always pinching things.

Why did Tigger go to the bathroom?
He wanted to find his friend Pooh!

Why do dragons sleep all day?
They like to hunt knights.

Why was the bee's hair sticky?
Because he used a honey-comb!

A horse walks into a bar. The bartender says, "Hey". The
horse replies, "Buddy, you read my mind!"

A leopard can never play hide and seek.
He's always spotted.

I just killed a huge spider running across the floor with my shoe. I don't care how big the spider is, no-one steals my shoe.

This shepherd said to me 'I've got 68 sheep. Would you like to round them up for me?' I said 'OK, you've got 70'.

My dog can do tricks.
It's a Labra-cadabra-dor.

What animal is always at a game of cricket?
A bat.

What do baby gorillas sleep in?
Apricots.

I wanted to buy a pet spider so I went to my pet shop but they were £70. I thought 'I can get one cheaper on the web'.

How do you make a goldfish age?
Take away the G.

I removed the shell from my racing snail to make him go faster but, if anything, it made him more sluggish.

I thought Tom Cruise was a boating holiday for male cats.

What always succeeds?
A budgie with no teeth.

What do you call a chicken that crosses the road, rolls in the dirt and crosses the road again? A dirty double-crossing chicken.

What do bumblebees chew?
Bumble gum.

Where do bees go to the bathroom?
The BP station

Why do bees hum?
Because they don't know the words.

Why do elephants have big ears?
Because Noddy wouldn't pay the ransom.

As a kid I was made to walk the plank.
We couldn't afford a dog.

What do you get if you sit under a cow?
A pat on the head.

What animal has more lives than a cat?
Frogs, they croak every day!

I can describe a hungry horse in four letters.
MTGG.

What animal needs to wear a wig?
A bald eagle!

**What did the pig say on a hot summer day?
I'm bacon.**

What do cats eat for breakfast?
Mice Krispies.

**What do you call two birds in love?
Tweethearts.**

What do you get if you cross a parrot with a shark?
A bird that will talk your ear off.

**What is a bird's favourite type of math?
Owl-gebra.**

What do birds say on Halloween?
"Trick or tweet!"

**Why do birds fly south in the winter?
Because it's too far to walk.**

Hedgehogs. Why can't they just share the hedge?

Why couldn't the pony sing?
She was a little horse.

Why do lions eat raw meat?
Because they never learned to cook.

Can one bird make a pun?
No but toucan.

How do rabbits travel?
By hare-plane.

What have 12 legs, 6 eyes, 3 tails and can't see?
Three blind mice.

**What do you call an alligator in a vest?
An investigator.**

What do you call a dinosaur that is sleeping?
A dino-snore!

**What did the judge say when he saw the skunk in the witness
box? "Odour in the court!"**

Why are fish so smart? Because they live in schools.

What's black, white and red all over?
A skunk with a nappy rash.

**What do you get when you cross a skunk with a chicken?
A fowl smell.**

A lorry load of tortoises has collided with a train load of terrapins. It was a turtle disaster.

What do you call a fish with no eyes?
A fsh.

Cats may think they're clean, but really they're just covered in cat spit.

How can you tell if an elephant has been in your refrigerator?
By the footprints in the butter!

Why did the pony get sent to his room? He wouldn't stop horsing around.

How do the fish get to school?
By octobus!

**Why do you never see a hippopotamus hiding in a tree?
Because they're really good at it.**

What do ducks watch on TV?
Duckumentaries.

What do you call a chicken at the North Pole?
Lost!

What do you call a fly without wings?
A walk.

What do you call a reindeer with bad manners?
RUDE-olph!

What goes up the river at 100 miles an hour?
A motor pike.

I went to the zoo and saw a loaf in a cage.
The zookeeper told me it was bread in captivity.

The best place to weigh whales is at a whale weigh station.

**What do you get when you cross a kangaroo with a sheep?
A woolly jumper.**

What cars do sheep like to drive? Lamborghinis.

Where do sheep go on vacation? The Baa-hamas.

What do you call a sheep with no legs?
A cloud

What do you call 100 sheep rolling down a hill?
A lamb-slide.

How do you make an octopus laugh?
With ten-tickles.

Do sheep count people when they go to sleep?

What creature is smarter than a talking parrot?
A spelling bee.

Thieves broke into the luxury home of a budgerigar cage millionaire.   They totally cleaned him out.

What did the buffalo say when his little boy left for school?
Bison

What did the fisherman say to the magician?
Pick up a cod, any cod.

What dinosaur had the best vocabulary?
The thesaurus.

My dog barks at everyone.
Still, what can you expect from a cross-breed?

How do you know if there's an elephant under your bed?
Your head hits the ceiling.

Do pigs use soap, or is that just hogwash?

I went on a holiday with my horse.
It was self-cantering.

Is someone who steals cats, dogs and other domestic animals
a petty criminal?

How do you catch a school of fish?
With a bookworm.

What do you call a chicken in a shell suit?
An egg.

What goes cluck, cluck, BOOM!?
A chicken in a minefield.

Why did the chicken cross the playground?
To get to the other slide!

Why did the rubber chicken cross the road?
To stretch her legs.

This chicken came up to me and said
'I can't find my eggs'.
I said 'You've probably mislaid them'.

What did one bee say to the other bee?
"I love bee-ing with you."

I used to run a dating agency for chickens,
but I was struggling to make hens meet.

What did the frog order at McDonald's?
French flies and Diet Croak.

What do you get if you cross a hedgehog with a giraffe?
A 10-foot tall toothbrush.

What do you get when dinosaurs crash their cars?
Tyrannosaurus wrecks.

What do you call a very fast llama?
Llamaghini!

What do you get when you cross a cow with a trampoline?
A milkshake!

What did the policeman use when he arrested the naughty pig? Ham-cuffs.

What did the sardine call the submarine?
A can of people!

What disease was the horse scared of getting?
Hay fever.

What do fish sing to each other?
Salmon-chanted evening!

What do you call a deer with 20/20 vision?
Good eye deer.

What do you sing to a kangaroo once a year?
Hoppy birthday.

What do you get if you cross a fish and an elephant?
Swimming trunks!

What do you give an elephant with diarrhoea?
Plenty of room.

Why are elephants so wrinkled?
Because they take too long to iron.

What do you call an elephant that
doesn't matter?
An irrelephant!

Why did the elephants get kicked out of the pool?
They kept dropping their trunks.

How do you raise a baby elephant?
With a forklift

My dog is a blacksmith!
Every time I open the front door, he makes a bolt for it.

What do you call a bear with no ears?
'B'

What do you say to a cow that crosses in front of your car?
Moooo-ve over.

What happened to the frog's car when his parking meter
expired? It got toad!

What happened when the frog's car broke down?
He jump started it.

What is a cow's favourite holiday?
Moo Year's Day.

What pie can fly?
A magpie.

When will the little snake arrive?
I don't know, but he won't be long.

What do you get if you cross a sheep with a dog?
A sheep that rounds itself up.

What do you call a bear with no teeth?
Gummy bear!

What do you call a blind dinosaur?
I-don't-think-he-saurus.

What's black and goes underground at 100 miles an hour?
A jet-propelled mole!

What fish is the brightest?
The sunfish.

105

What has two grey legs and two brown legs?
An elephant with diarrhoea.

What kind of shoes do frogs wear?
Open toad.

When does a horse talk?
Only whinney wants to!

Why was the horse so happy?
Because he lived in a stable environment.

What kind of food do race horses like to eat?
Fast food.

Which type of cheese do horses like best?
Masc-a-pony

Why do cowboys ride horses?
Because they're too heavy to carry.

What do you call a cow with no legs?
Ground beef!

What is a dolphin's favourite TV show?
Whale of fortune!

What goes clip?
A one-legged horse.

What would you call a sleeping bull?
A bulldozer

Where do animals go when their tails fall off?
The retail store.

Why do cows have bells?
Because their horns don't work.

Why was Tigger looking in the toilet?
He was looking for Pooh.

Why was the mother firefly so happy?
Because all her children were so bright.

Why did the parrot wear a raincoat?
So he could be polyunsaturated.

Why didn't the dog want to play football?
Because it was a boxer.

Why do gorillas have big nostrils?
Because they have big fingers.

What is the best thing to do if a bull charges you?
Pay the bull.

Why don't koalas count as bears?
They don't have the right koala-fications.

Where do cows come from?
Cattle-logs.

What do you call a deer with no eyes?
No eye deer.

Graham Cann

Where do dogs park?
In a barking lot.

What kind of animal is always at a baseball game?
A bat!

What lies on the ground 100 feet in the air?
A dead centipede.

What was the first animal to go into space?
The cow that jumped over the moon!

What's black and white and red all over?
An embarrassed zebra.

When is a man like a snake?
When he's rattled.

Where do fish keep their money?
In the river bank!

Where do young cows eat lunch?
In a calf-ateria!

Where do rabbits go after they get married?
On a bunny-moon!

What musical keys do cows sing in?
Beef flat

What kind of pillar can't hold up a building?
A caterpillar.

What time do ducks wake up?
At the quack of dawn.

What sound do hedgehogs make when they hug?
Ouch!

What's the difference between a fish and a piano?
You can't tuna fish!

What's the definition of a slug?
A homeless snail.

Where do cows go for entertainment?
To the moo-vies.

Why could Long John Silver never find an aspirin?
Because his parrots ate 'em all.

How do you fit more pigs on your farm?
Build a sty-scraper.

Why did the turtle cross the road?
To get to the shell station!

Why did the spider go to the computer?
To check out his website.

Why don't penguins fly?
They're not tall enough to be pilots.

How do you count a herd of cattle?
With a cowculator.

Why don't sheep shrink when it rains?

Why do sharks swim in salt water?
Because pepper water makes them sneeze!

Why do tigers have stripes?
So they won't be spotted.

Why don't crabs give to charity?
Because they're shellfish.

Why can't dogs drive?
They can't find a barking space.

**Why did the chewing gum cross the road?
It was stuck to the leg of a chicken**

Why did the starfish cross the road?
To get to the other tide!

**Why didn't the duck pay for the lip balm?
He wanted to put it on his bill.**

Why do ducks watch the news?
To get the feather forecast.

**Why did the hedgehog cross the road?
To see his flatmate.**

What do you call a pig with three eyes?
A piiig!

Why can't you play hockey with pigs?
They always hog the puck.

Why don't snails fart?
Because their houses don't have any windows.

Why is a fish easy to weigh?
Because it has its own scales!

Why is Turtle Wax so expensive?
Because turtles have such tiny ears.

What kind of car does Micky Mouse's wife drive?
A Minnie van.

Why should you never trust a pig with a secret?
Because it's bound to squeal!

What do you call a dinosaur at the rodeo?
A bronco-saurus.

What do you call a gorilla with a banana in each ear?
Anything you like. He can't hear you.

What do you call a frog stuck in mud?
Unhoppy.

What do you call a snake who works for the British
Government?
A civil serpent.

What do you call an ant who fights crime?
A vagilanty

What do you call a little amphibian who never goes out?
Hermit the Frog.

What do you call a duck that gets all A's? A wise quacker.

My talking dog gave me a stick the other day and told me he found it 600 miles away. That's a bit far-fetched!

What goes tick, tick, woof, woof?
A watch dog!

What do you get when you cross a cow and a lawnmower?
A lawnmooer.

What do you say to a frog that needs a ride? Hop in.

What do you get when you cross a centipede with a parrot?
A walkie talkie.

What does a spider's bride wear?
A webbing dress!

What has 100 legs, 25 noses and is very loud?
A herd of stampeding hippos.

What do you call a pig that knows karate?
A pork chop!

What do you call a dinosaur that wears a cowboy hat and boots? Tyrannosaurus Tex.

What do you call a dinosaur with bad vision?
A Do-you-think-he-saurus!

What do you call a dog with no legs?
It doesn't matter what you call it, it's not going to come.

What do you call a donkey with three legs and one eye?
A winky wonkey.

A cross between a donkey and a motorcycle is known as a Yam-Hee-Haw.

A TICKET TO RIDE

What do you call it
when a giraffe swallows a toy jet?
A plane in the neck

What do you get when you cross a snake and a plane?
A Boeing Constrictor.

If an electric train is travelling south, which way is the smoke going? There is no smoke. It's an electric train!

How do all the oceans say hello to each other?
They wave.

What did one volcano say to the other volcano? "I lava you!"

What do you call a flying policeman?
A heli-copper

What has four wheels and flies? A garbage truck!

What did the farmer say when he lost his tractor?
"Where's my tractor?"

Where do pencils go on vacation?
Pencil-vania.

When is a car not a car?
When it turns into a parking space.

Crime in multi-storey car parks.
That's wrong on so many levels.

I asked someone at the bus stop how long the next bus would
be? He said 'About thirty feet.'

What do you call a train loaded with toffee?
A chew-chew train.

What's the difference between a teacher and a train?
Teacher says "Spit your gum out".
The train says "Chew Chew".

How do mountains stay warm in winter?
Snowcaps.

What has one horn and gives milk? A milk tanker.

How did the egg get up the mountain?
He scrambled up.

30% of car accidents in Sweden involve a moose.
I say don't let them drive.

If you threw a white stone into the Red Sea, what would it become?
Wet.

What did the traffic lights say to the car?
Look away, I'm about to change!

I recently went on a barging holiday. I haven't got a boat.
I just kept barging into people.

How do you make a Swiss Roll? Push him down a mountain.

How do you pay for parking in space?
A parking meteor.

If everyone bought a white car, what would we have?
A white carnation.

What did the beach say when the tide came in?
Long time, no sea.

What goes through towns and over hills but never moves?
A road.

Jack rode into town on Friday and rode out two days later on
Friday. How can that be possible?
Friday is the name of his horse.

What's green, has two legs and a trunk?
A seasick tourist.

What is able to travel around the globe, but stays in the corner the whole time? A stamp.

What is brown, hairy and wears sunglasses?
A coconut on vacation.

When do astronauts eat?
Launch time.

What did the policeman say to his tummy?
Freeze! You're under a vest!

Where can you find cities, towns, shops, and streets but no people? On a map.

Three men in a boat. It capsized but only two got their hair wet. Why? One of them was bald.

I've just been on a once-in-a-lifetime holiday.
Never again!

What did the sink say to the toilet?
You look really flushed!

What do you call a person who used to like tractors?
An extractor fan.

What ship has two mates but no captain?
A relationship.

What do you call a Spanish man who has lost his car?
Carlos.

What do you do with old German cars?
Take 'em to the old Volk's home.

Have you heard about the magic tractor?
It turned into a field.

What kind of car does a farmer drive?
A cornvertable.

Where does a mountain climber keep his plane?
In a cliffhanger.

Why is the Mississippi such an unusual river?
It has four eyes and it can't even see!

Why couldn't the bicycle stand up for itself?
It was two-tyred.

What do you get when you cross a fly, a car, and a dog?
A flying carpet!

Where do bees go on their holiday?
Stingapore!

A MAD, MAD WORLD

What do you get when you cross a snowman and a vampire?
Frostbite!

Where does a snowman keep his money? A snow bank.

What do you call an old snowman?
Water.

How do you get a ghost to lie perfectly flat?
Use a spirit level.

What do ghosts avoid?
The living room.

What do ghosts like to eat in the summer?
I scream.

What do you call a ghost's true love.
His ghoul-friend.

Why are ghosts such bad liars?
Because you can see right through them!

Why do ghosts love elevators?
It lifts their spirits.

A librarian slipped and fell on the library floor.
It was the non-friction section.

Did you hear about the kidnapping at school?
He woke up.

How can you make seven even?
Remove the "S".

How many books can you put into an empty backpack?
One - after that it's not empty.

How many letters are in The Alphabet? There are 11 letters in
The Alphabet.

I asked the librarian if they had any books on pantomimes. She
said 'They're behind you'.

What begins with a T, ends with a T and has T in it?
A teapot.

How do astronomers organise a party.
They planet.

How do you stop an astronaut's baby from crying?
You rocket.

I've got a chronic fear of giants —
Fee-fi-phobia!

How does the moon cut his hair?
Eclipse it!

They come out at night without being called and are lost in the day without being stolen. What are they?
Stars.

What does a cloud wear under his raincoat?
Thunderwear.

Why didn't the sun go to college? He already had a million degrees.

Why did the farmer plough his field with a steamroller?
He wanted to grow mashed potatoes.

Why did the girl throw butter out of the window?
To see butter-fly.

Why did the firefly get bad grades in school?
He wasn't very bright!

How do trees get on the internet?
They log in!

How do you cut the sea in half?
With a see saw!

I have no legs. I will never walk but always run. What am I?
A river.

I've heard the Incredible Hulk is a good gardener.
He's got green fingers.

What did the big flower say to the little flower?
"Hi bud".

What do you call a flower that runs on electricity?
A power plant.

What do you call a funny mountain?
Hill-arious!

What has ears but cannot hear?
A cornfield.

What is full of holes but still holds water?
A sponge.

What kind of room has no doors or windows?
A mushroom.

What kind of tree can you carry in your hand?
A palm.

What's brown and runs round a field?
A fence.

What's brown and sticky?
A stick.

How do you learn to be a trash collector?
Just pick it up as you go along.

How do you make a tissue dance?
Put a little boogey in it!

How do you make a Venetian blind?
Stick a finger in its eye.

How do you make the number one disappear?
Add the letter G and it's 'gone'.

How many months have 28 days?
All of them.

I am full of keys but I cannot open any door. What am I?
A piano.

What did the digital clock say to the grandfather clock?
Look! No hands!

I don't like my hands. I always keep them at arm's length.

What has two legs but can't walk?
A pair of jeans.

Why should you always avoid tornado chasers?
Because they're always passing wind.

What has two hands, a round face, always runs, but stays in
one place? A clock.

How do you talk to a giant?
Use big words.

I tried to smuggle a wild animal out of Australia.
But it Dingo as planned.

What has four legs but can't walk?
A table.

What has one head, one foot and four legs?
A bed.

6:30 is the best time of day. Hands down!

David's father had three sons: Snap, Crackle and? David!

I am a word. If you pronounce me rightly, it will be wrong. If
you pronounce me wrong, it is right. What word am I?
Wrong.

I bought a microwave bed recently. 8 hours sleep in 10 minutes!

I can be cracked, I can be made. I can be told, I can be played. What am I? A joke.

I do not speak and cannot hear but will always tell the truth. What am I? A mirror.

I have a head and a tail but no body. What am I? A coin.

Germinate - is to become a naturalised German.

Have you tried that new 007 glue? It Bonds in seconds.

If two is company and three is a crowd, what are four and five? Nine.

My kids are seven and five. We couldn't think of better names.

Name three days consecutively where none of the seven days of the week appear? Yesterday, Today and Tomorrow.

Two tons of human hair destined for a wig maker has been stolen. Police are combing the area.

What day of the week are most twins born on? Twos-Day.

What do you call two guys hanging on a window? Kurt and Rod.

What has one eye, but can't see? A needle.

What do you call two witches living together? Broom-mates.

I invented a cold air balloon, but it didn't really take off.

Why can't a hand be 12 inches long?
Because then it would be a foot!

You draw a line. Without touching it, how do you make the line longer? You draw a shorter line next to it and then it becomes the longer line.

Why was 6 afraid of 7? Because 7, 8, 9!

I recently got crushed by a pile of books but I suppose I only have my shelf to blame.

What do elves learn in school? The elf-abet.

The lad who sat next to me at school one day ate his calculator. Everybody said he was a weirdo but like I said 'It's what's inside him that counts'.

What goes 99 thump?
An ice cream man being mugged.

What do you call someone who refuses to fart in public?
A private tooter.

What do you get when you cross a vampire and a teacher?
Lots of blood tests!

Why did the student eat his homework?
Because the teacher said it was a piece of cake!

Why did the teacher put on sunglasses? Because her students
were so bright.

What is the longest word in the dictionary? Smiles because
there is a mile between each 's'.

What's a pirate's favourite letter? Arrgghhhh!

Which pirate drools continuously? Long John Saliva.

Why couldn't the pirate learn the alphabet? Because he was always lost at "C".

Why did the old man fall down the well? Because he couldn't see that well.

What did one firefly say to the other?
I've got to glow now.

Why did the boy throw a clock out the window?
To see time fly.

What's yellow on the inside and green on the outside?
A banana dressed up as a cucumber.

What do you call Batman and Robin after they've been run over by a steamroller?
Flatman and Ribbon.

Why did the boy bring a ladder to school?
Because he thought it was a high school!

How much do pirates charge to pierce someone's ear?
A Buck an ear!

My girlfriend ditched me for a fisherman.
I was gutted.

What do you call a boy named Lee that no one talks to?
Lonely.

Why did the boy bury his torch?
Because the batteries died.

I'm not a very muscular man.
The strongest thing about me is my password.

Where's Spiderman's home page?
On the worldwide web.

Did you hear the joke about the roof?
Never mind, it's over your head.

Did you know Peter Pan had a brother called Deep?

Everyone has one and no-one can lose it. What is it?
Your shadow.

I'm really into grandfather clocks – big time.

If I have it, I don't share it. If I share it, I don't have it.
What is it?
A secret.

I've got a front door made of sponge.
Don't knock it!

If you don't keep me, I break. What am I? A promise.

My teacher said to me 'Do you think there's life on Mars?' I said 'Without a doubt. I can see at least two wasps round the wrapper'.

The only way prisoners can call each other is on cell phones.

Police have just arrested the world tongue twister champion.
I imagine he'll be given a tough sentence.

What do lawyers wear to court? Lawsuits.

What do you call a knight who is afraid to fight?
Sir Render.

I'm with poor people and rich people don't have me. If you eat me, you will die. What am I? Nothing.

What do you call a man sweeping up leaves?
Russell.

What does a vampire take for a sore throat?
Coffin drops.

What do you call a droid that takes the long way round?
R2 detour.

Did you hear about the anti-social media site?
It's called 'Shut-yer-facebook'.

What do you call an underwater spy?
James Pond.

What do mermaids have on toast? Mermerlade.

What are hippies?
Something to hang your leggies on.

What do you call a guy lying on your doorstep? Matt.

What do you call Dracula with hay fever?
The Pollen Count.

How do ghosts wash their hair?
With sham-boo!

Why are pirates so mean?
They just aarrrrrr!

Why did the vampire give up acting?
He couldn't find a part he could get his teeth into.

What is a witch's favourite subject?
Spelling.

Why did Darth Vader turn off one light?
He prefers it on the dark side.

Why were they called the Dark Ages?
Because there were lots of knights.

What goes Oh, Oh, Oh?
Santa walking backwards.

Why did the robber have a bath?
He wanted to make a clean getaway.

Why was the Maths book sad? It had too many problems.

Why did the pianist bang their head against the keys?
They were playing by ear.

What object is the king of the classroom? The ruler!

Why did the man put his money in the freezer? He wanted
cold, hard cash!

Why couldn't the sailors play cards?
The captain was standing on the deck.

What did one wall say to the other? I'll meet you at the corner.

Why did the man run around his bed?
He was trying to catch up on his sleep!

151

I refuse to work down a coal mine. It's beneath me.

I had to quit my job at the shoe recycling factory.
It was sole destroying.

**What do cannibals have for lunch?
Baked beings.**

I just watched a documentary on the uses of the pick axe.
It was ground breaking stuff.

**I was a war baby. My parents took one look at me and started
fighting.**

What did the grape do when it was crushed?
It let out a little whine.

**I was up all night wondering what happened to the sun and
suddenly it dawned on me.**

What did the birthday balloon say to the pin?
"Hi, Buster".

My next-door neighbour's kid has an imaginary drum kit.
You can't beat that!

What do you call a boomerang that won't come back?
A stick!

What five letter word becomes shorter when you add two
letters to it? Short.

What goes up but never goes down?
Your age.

What is a computer's favourite snack?
Computer chips!

I will always come but never arrive today.
What am I? Tomorrow.

Graham Cann

I'm glad I know sign language.
It could come in handy.

Someone left some plasticine at my home yesterday.
I don't know what to make of it.

I'm totally deaf.
I never thought I'd hear myself say that.

What did the big chimney say to the little chimney?
You're too young to smoke.

What breaks when you say it?
Silence.

What did the blanket say to the bed?
Don't worry, I've got you covered.

What does a house wear?
An address.

What did the hat say to the scarf?
You hang around and I'll go on ahead.

What do you call a very popular perfume?
A best-smeller.

What falls in winter but never gets hurt?
Snow.

What gets bigger and bigger as you take more away from it?
A hole.

What gets wetter the more it dries?
A towel.

What goes up a chimney when down, but cannot go down the chimney when up? An umbrella.

What has a neck but no head?
A bottle.

What is a light year?
The same as a regular year, but with fewer calories.

What has many rings but no fingers? A telephone.

What occurs once in a minute, twice in a moment and never in a thousand years?
a thousand years?
The letter M.

What did the elevator say when he sneezed?
I'm coming down with something.

What has a thumb and four fingers, but is not alive?
A glove.

Which hand is it better to write with?
Neither, it's better to write with a pencil.

What sounds like a sneeze and is made of leather?
A shoe!

Why didn't the teddy bear eat dessert?
Because he was stuffed.

Why was the broom running late?
It over-swept.

What is something you'll never see again?
Yesterday.

What kind of music do mummies listen to?
Wrap music.

What is next in this sequence? JFMAMJJASON......
The letter D. The sequence contains the first letter of each month.

What is a tornado's favourite game to play?
Twister.

What do you call a smelly fairy?
Stinkerbell.

What starts with E, ends with E and only has one letter in it?
An envelope.

What is the centre of gravity?
The letter V.

There were two tomatoes walking down the road.
Which one was the cowboy? Neither, they were both redskins.

What's brown and sounds like a bell?
Dung!

What question do you never answer "yes" to?
"Are you asleep?"

When is a door not a door?
When it's ajar.

What's the difference between a jeweller and a jailer? A
jeweller sells watches. A jailer watches cells.

When you look for something, why is it always in the last place you look? Because when you find it, you stop looking.

Where does Friday come before Thursday?
In a dictionary.

Which weighs more - a pound of feathers or a pound of bricks?
Neither, they both weigh one pound!

Which letter of the alphabet has the most water?
C.

Which word in the dictionary is spelt incorrectly?
Incorrectly.

Why can't Elsa have a balloon?
Because she'll let it go.

Who did the computer call when it was in trouble?
The screen-saver.

Why did the belt go to jail?
Because he held up a pair of pants.

Whoever coined the phrase 'Quiet as a mouse' has never stepped on one.

What did the chewing gum say to the shoe?
I'm stuck on you.

Why are shoemakers such kind people?
Because they have good soles.

Why did the book join the police?
He wanted to go undercover.

Why did the picture go to prison?
Because it had been framed.

Why is a bad joke like a bad pencil?
It has no point!

Why did the computer go to the opticians?
It needed to improve its 'web-sight'.

Why is it so windy inside an arena?
All those fans!

A boy walked into a pet shop and asked to buy a wasp.
The shopkeeper said "We don't sell wasps."
The boys said "You do! There's one in the window."

Why is an island like the letter T?
Because it's in the middle of water.

What do you call a clumsy bee that drops things?
A fumble-bee.

What's the difference between a post box and an elephant's
bottom? You don't know?
That's the last time I ask you to post a letter!

EGG-STRA FUN

I threw a biscuit at my neighbour the other day but he ducked.
Jammy dodger!

People buy me to eat but never eat me. What am I? A plate.

How do you fix a broken tomato?
With tomato paste.

What did the gingerbread man put under his blankets?
A cookie sheet.

What do you call a peanut in a spacesuit? An astronut!

What do you get when you cross a sweet potato and a jazz
musician? A yam session.

What sound does a nut make when it sneezes?
CASHEW!

Why did the melon jump in the lake?
Because she wanted to be a watermelon.

What's orange and sounds like a parrot?
A carrot.

Where do burgers like to dance?
A meatball.

What has to be broken before you can use it?
An egg.

What's worse than finding a worm in your apple?
Finding half a worm.

What type of cheese is made backwards?
Edam.

Why do mushrooms get invited to all the parties?
Because they are fungis.

Where do you learn to make ice-cream?
At sundae school.

What do you give a
sick lemon?
Lemon aid

What do you call a fruit that goes into space?
A coco-naut!

How do you mend a broken pumpkin?
With a pumpkin patch.

Why did the tomato blush?
Because he saw the salad dressing.

What did the pirate order when he went to a fish restaurant!
Pieces of skate.

What Jedi can you eat?
Obi Wan Cannoli!

A sandwich walked into a bar. The barman said 'Sorry we don't
serve food in here'.

Most pizza jokes are pretty cheesy.

What did the hamburger give to her sweetheart?
An onion ring.

I'm on a seafood diet. Every time I see food, I eat it.

Did you hear about the restaurant on the moon?
The food was good but there was no atmosphere.

What do you call a runaway pea?
An esca-pea.

What did the egg say to the other egg?
Let's get cracking.

Why do bananas have to put on sunscreen before they go to the beach? In case they peel!

What's smelly, round and laughs?
A tickled onion.

How does a cucumber become a pickle?
It goes through a jarring experience.

My friend drowned in a bowl of muesli. He was pulled in by a strong currant.

What does bread do on vacation? Loaf around.

Why was the baby strawberry crying?
Because her parents were in a jam.

What was the reporter doing at the ice cream shop?
Getting the scoop.

What happened when the rhubarb was arrested?
It was kept in custardy.

What did one plate say to the other? Dinner's on me!

What did the microwave say to the other microwave?
Is it me or is it really hot in here?

What is fast, loud and crunchy?
A rocket chip.

Why did the orange lose the race? It ran out of juice.

What did baby corn say to mama corn?
"Where's popcorn?"

What do you call a fake noodle?
An impasta!

Why is Europe like a frying pan?
Because it has Greece at the bottom.

What room is impossible to enter? A mushroom.

What do you get if you cross a soldier and a chilli?
A pepperarmy.

Alphabet spaghetti warning: 'May contain N U T S'.

How do you make an apple puff?
Chase it round the garden.

Did you know it takes 40 pigs to make 4,000 sausages?
It's amazing what you can teach them.

How do you make a hotdog stand?
Take away its chair?

THE FIT-BIT

Which top football team's favourite food is ice-cream?
Aston Vanilla

A karate instructor was arrested after leaving the shop.
He was charged with chop lifting.

"Doctor, Doctor I feel like a window." "Tell me where the pane is."

A man knocked on my door asking for a small donation for the local swimming pool. So I gave him a glass of water.

What is harder to catch the faster you run?
Your breath.

Standing in a park, I was wondering why a Frisbee gets larger the closer it gets. And then it hit me.

"Doctor, Doctor, what's good for excessive wind?"
" A kite."

Why do people go to a baseball stadium on a hot day?
Because it's full of fans.

Measles. Now that's a rash thing to say.

My friend's breath is so bad,
his dentist will only treat him over the phone".

Why did the scuba divers laugh when they got near the coral reef? Because they saw a clownfish.

What race is never run? A swimming race.

A man went to see an eye doctor. The receptionist asked him what was wrong. He said "I keep seeing spots in front of my eyes". She said "Have you seen a doctor?" He said "No, just spots".

The world's worst boxer has finally put his life story on You Tube. He's had one million hits.

This joke is about people with crooked teeth.
Brace yourself!

How does a scientist freshen her breath? With experi-mints!

What's a horses favorite sport?
Stable tennis.

I broke my leg when I tripped over a box of paper towels last night, but the doctor said it was only tissue damage.

What's red and bad for your teeth? A brick.

Can you spell rotted with two letters? DK (decay).

When is a doctor most annoyed? When he is out of patients.

Why did the retired soccer player need a lighter?
Because he didn't have any more matches.

What can you catch but never throw? A cold

"Doctor, Doctor, I'm convinced I'm a wheelbarrow."
"You shouldn't let anyone push you around."

Why did the tap dancer retire? He kept falling in the sink.

What musical instrument is found in the bathroom?
A tuba toothpaste.

Bobby throws a ball as hard as he can. It comes back to him
even though nothing and nobody touches it.
How? He throws it straight up.

Why did the karate master rob the shoe shop? Just for kicks.

Patient: "Doctor, I think I'm a cat". Doctor: "How long's this
been going on?" Patient: "Since I was a kitten".

Why is it that your nose runs but your feet smell?

Why is Cinderella bad at soccer?
Because she runs away from the ball.

Why did the cupboard learn karate?
For shelf-defence.

Why do golfers take an extra pair of socks?
In case they get a hole in one!

What tastes better than it smells? A tongue.

What did the leg bone say to the foot?
Stick with me and you'll go places.

Why do basketball players love doughnuts?
Because they can dunk 'em!

How are false teeth like stars?
They come out at night.

What did one toe say to the other?
See you toe-morrow.

What do you call a man with a rubber toe?
Roberto.

What musical instrument is found in the bathroom?
A tuba toothpaste.

Why was the weightlifter frustrated?
He was surrounded by dumbbells.

Dentistry can be such a depressing job.
You're always looking down in the mouth.

How did the barber win the cross country race?
He took a short cut.

Why did the opera singer go sailing?
She wanted to hit the high C's.

I rushed to hospital today to see my uncle who'd been run over by a steamroller. 'Yes' explained the nurse. 'He's in Room 21...........22 and 23'.

Why was the nose sad? Because it didn't get picked.

What kind of award did the dentist receive?
A little plaque.

What's faster: hot or cold?
Hot, because everyone catches a cold.

Where do hungry football players play?
In the Supper Bowl.

"Doctor, Doctor, I keep thinking I'm a clock."
"Try not to get wound up."

What did the nose say to the finger?
Stop picking on me!

"Doctor, Doctor, I keep thinking I'm a pair of curtains."
"Pull yourself together."

What's the least honest bone in the body?
The fibula.

"Doctor, Doctor, I think I'm a dog". "Okay have a seat." "I can't, I'm not allowed on the furniture."

I once met a hippo that had a sinus infection. I named it 'The heap-o-snotamus.'

"Doctor, Doctor I've got a lettuce sticking out of my ear!"
"Unfortunately, it looks like the tip of the iceberg."

What did the skeleton order for dinner?
Spare ribs.

Why didn't the skeleton go to the dance?

Because he had nobody to go with!

What did one eye say to the other?
Between us, something smells.

QUIZZ~WHIZZ

Q. What are the only two countries in the world where you can't buy Coca Cola?

A. *North Korea and Cuba.*

Q. How do you tell the age of a horse?
A. *By its teeth.*

Q. How many colours are there in a rainbow?
A. *Seven. Red, orange, yellow, green, blue, indigo and violet.*

Q. What's the biggest planet in our solar system?
A. *Jupiter. It's twice as big as all the other planets combined.*

Q. How fast was the first person convicted of speeding going?
A. *8 miles per hour, in 1896.*

Q. How many years old is the oldest piece of chewing gum?
A. *5,000 years.*

Q. What do you call a group of giraffes?
A. *A tower.*

Q. What is the biggest bone on the human body?
A. *The thigh bone or femur.*

Q. How long did the longest bout of hiccups last?
A. *68 years!*

Q. How many Earths could fit inside the sun?
A. *One million.*

Q. How many rings make up the symbol for the Olympic Games?   A. *Five.*

Q. How many noses does a slug have?
A. *Four.*

Q. What is Shrek's wife's name?
A. *Fiona.*

Q. What is the fastest bird and how fast can it fly?
A. *The peregrine falcon.*
It can fly at a speed of 168-217 miles per hour.

Q. What has hands but can't clap?
A. *A clock.*

Q. What is the fastest aquatic animal?
A. *The Sailfish. It can reach speeds of 68mph.*

Q. What was the first living creature to go into space?
A. *A dog named Laika.*

Q. What is the smallest ocean in the world?
A. *The Arctic.*

Q. What is the largest ocean in the world?
A. *The Pacific.*

Q. What is the fastest land animal?
A. *The cheetah. It can hit speeds of up to 70 miles per hour.*

Q. What is the fear of long words known as?
A. *Hippopotomostrosesquippedaliophobia.*

Q. What is the world record for the number of hot dogs eaten in one sitting?
A. *76 in 10 minutes.*

Q. What land animal can open its mouth the widest?
A. *The hippopotamus. It can open its jaws to around 1.2 metres (4 feet).*

Q. What were clocks missing before 1577?
A. *Minute hands.*

Q. What's the largest animal on Earth?
A. *The blue whale. It can weigh up to 200 tons.*

Q. Which fruit does Spongebob live in?
A. *A pineapple.*

Q. Which famous singer was involved in composing the music for Sonic the Hedgehog 3?
A. *Michael Jackson.*

Q. What is the most struggling of all subjects because it is full of problems?
A. *Mathematics.*

Q. Most kids love to carry these keys. What are they?
A. *Cookies.*

Graham Cann

WOWZER!?!

Did you know it's illegal to name your pig Napoleon in France?

Did you know it's illegal
for a chicken to cross the road in Quitman, Georgia US?

Did you know
in Vermont US, women must obtain written permission from
their husbands to wear false teeth?

Did you know
bubble wrap was originally invented as wallpaper?

Did you know
cats cannot taste anything that's sweet?

Did you know
as well as having unique finger prints,
we all have unique tongue prints?

Did you know it's illegal
to take a lion to the cinema in Baltimore, US?

Did you know
a hippopotomus produces pink milk?

Did you know it's illegal
to wear a suit of armor in British Parliament?

Did you know it's illegal
to sell cornflakes on a Sunday in Columbus, Ohio US?

Did you know
you can be fined for building sand castles in Magaluf, Majorca?

Did you know
a 70 year old woman once completed seven marathons in
seven days, across seven continents?

Did you know it's illegal to pass wind in Malawi?

Did you know
in 1913 parents could mail their kids to grandma's
through the postal service in the US?

Did you know it's illegal to
have a sleeping donkey in your bathtub after 7pm in Arizona
US?

Did you know
Bill Gates has donated nearly half of his fortune?

Did you know it's illegal
to ski down a mountain in Switzerland while reciting poetry?

Did you know, in England
it's illegal to handle salmon in suspicious circumstances?

**Did you know it's illegal
to wrestle a bear in South Africa?**

Did you know
bees are found everywhere in the world apart from Antarctica?

**Did you know
if a donkey and a zebra have a baby, it's called a zonkey?**

Did you know
cows moo with regional accents?

**Did you know it's illegal
to wear a fake mustache in an Alabama church?**

Did you know
if you eat too many carrots you'll turn orange?

**Did you know Monks
in Tibet are banned from reincarnating without permission?**

Did you know it's illegal
to carry ice cream cones in your pocket in Kentucky US?

**Did you know it's illegal
for a single woman to skydive on a Sunday in Florida US?**

Did you know
glass balls can bounce higher than rubber ones?

**Did you know
it's illegal to sell chewing gum in Singapore?**

Did you know
it's impossible for most people to lick their own elbow?

**Did you know
it's illegal to drive blindfolded in Alabama US?**

Did you know
the wood frog can hold its pee for up to eight months?

**Did you know
the Queen owns all the swans in England?**

Did you know
it's illegal to lick toads in California US?

**Did you know
snails can sleep for 3 years?**

Did you know
goats have rectangular pupils in their eyes?

**Did you know it's illegal
to ride an ugly horse in Wilbur, Washington US?**

Did you know
McDonalds once made bubblegum-flavoured broccoli?

**Did you know
the Taj Mahal in India is made entirely from marble?**

Did you know
giraffe tongues can be 20 inches long?

**Did you know the average time for plastic bottles to
decompose is 450 years while glass bottles take 1,000,000
years?**

Did you know you can be fined for playing with
silly string in public places in Southington, Connecticut US?

Did you know
cows can walk upstairs but not down them on their own?

Did you know sharks can live for five centuries?

Did you know
the smallest country in the world takes up 0.44 square kilometres -Vatican City, an independent state surrounded by Rome?

Did you know
there was a prehistoric dragonfly whose wings spanned more than two feet?

Did you know
the number four is the only number with the same amount of letters?

Did you know
it's impossible for a pig to look up into the sky?

Did you know in Tuszyn, Poland, officials opposed naming a park after Winnie the Pooh because he's half naked?

Did you know
your nose and ears continue to get bigger even when the rest
of you has stopped?

WOULD YOU BE GOOD ENOUGH TO DO ME A BIG FAVOUR?

I hope very much that you enjoyed this book. I would be very grateful if you could leave a review for '1001 Jokes 4 Kids' on Amazon. The more positive the reviews, the more people will be encouraged to take a look at this book and, hopefully, get their kids laughing too!

Many thanks!

ACKNOWLEDGMENTS

Whilst this book may have my name as author, I owe a huge debt of gratitude to my wife, Jules, who has worked tirelessly on the manuscript for this book. She has also been instrumental in providing many of the funnies and trivia, not forgetting the formatting and all the illustrations.

A selection of books from the same publisher:

For the full range, please visit

https://www.chascannco.com

For more information, please scan the QR code below the books of your choice.

COLOURING BOOKS FOR ALL AGES

COLOUR 'N COUNT FIRST COLOURING BOOK

The perfect way for your child to learn, build vocabulary and help develop their individual creativity.

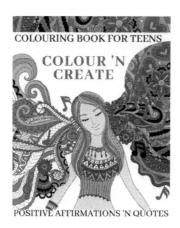

COLOUR 'N CREATE

Reconnect to your inner creativity, colouring your way to inner peace and calm (for teens).

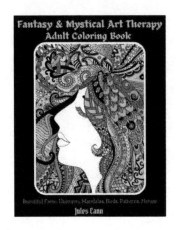

FANTASY AND MYSTICAL ART THERAPY

Enter a world of fantasy and mysticism to help you relax, unwind and exercise your imagination.

HUMOUR

1001 JOKE BOOK SERIES

Thousands of hilarious one-liners and dad jokes (Suitable for ages 13+)

LIFESTYLE

MINDFULNESS FOR BEGINNERS

An ideal mindfulness guide for beginners with exercises to help calm your mind and bring peace and contentment into your life.

THE NEW PUPPY HANDBOOK

Your easy step-by-step guide to choosing, training and caring for your puppy.

Printed in Great Britain
by Amazon

29199255R00121